LEAVING MY HOMELAND

After the Journey

Returning to Guatemala

CRABTREE
PUBLISHING COMPANY
WWW.CRABTREEBOOKS.COM

Heather C. Hudak

CRABTREE
PUBLISHING COMPANY
WWW.CRABTREEBOOKS.COM

Author: Heather C. Hudak

Editors: Sarah Eason, Harriet McGregor, and Janine Deschenes

Proofreader and indexer: Wendy Scavuzzo

Editorial director: Kathy Middleton

Design: Paul Myerscough and Jessica Moon

Cover design: Samara Parent

Photo research: Rachel Blount

**Production coordinator and
  Prepress technician:** Ken Wright

Print coordinator: Katherine Berti

Consultants: Hawa Sabriye and HaEun Kim, Centre for Refugee Studies,
  York University

Produced for Crabtree Publishing Company by Calcium Creative

Publisher's Note: The story presented in this book is a fictional account
based on extensive research of real-life accounts by refugees, with the aim
of reflecting the true experience of refugee children and their families.

Photo Credits:
t=Top, c=Center, b=Bottom, l= Left, r=Right

Inside: Flickr: Adam Jones: p. 4c; Shutterstock: Abeadev: p. 7tl; AndriyA:
p. 16t; Asanru: p. 13; Bumihills: p. 26t; Rob Crandall: pp. 19c, 24c;
Elenabsl: pp. 10t, 11r; Great Vector Elements: p. 11tr; Francisco
Sandoval Guate: p. 24b; Tatiana Gulyaeva: p. 25cr; Charles Harker:
p. 22t; Isovector: p. 19b; Helga Khorimarko: pp. 11tl, 18t; KittyVector:
p. 5t; Janos Levente: p. 15t; Light S: p. 23t; LineTale: p. 18c; Macrovector: p.
28b; Maxx-Studio: p. 4tl; Meunierd: pp. 6–7b, 22b; Mspoint: p. 28t; Byron
Ortiz: pp. 8c, 18b, 19t, 20, 21, 23c; Matyas Rehak: pp. 16–17b; Assaf Ben
Shoshan: p. 27; Ulrike Stein: p. 12; Sudowoodo: pp. 17b, 29t; Sunflowerr:
p. 4tr; SunshineVector: p. 3; Olivier Tabary: p. 26b; Shawn Talbot: p. 11c;
Tateyama: p. 16c; What's My Name: p. 15b; Murat Irfan Yalcin: p. 25b;
Zzveillust: p. 6tr; UNHCR: © UNHCR/Santiago Escobar-Jaramillo:
p. 10; © UNHCR/Tito Herrera: pp. 8–9b; © UNHCR/Betty Press: pp.
14–15b; © UNHCR/R. Ramirez: p. 28; © UNHCR/A. Serrano: pp. 14–15t;
© UNHCR/Daniele Volpe: pp. 6–7c; Wikimedia Commons: U.S. Army
photo by Sgt. Austin Berner: p. 29c.

Cover: Shutterstock: Olivier Tabary.

Library and Archives Canada Cataloguing in Publication

Hudak, Heather C., 1975-, author
        Returning to Guatemala / Heather C. Hudak.

(Leaving my homeland : after the journey)
Includes index.
Issued in print and electronic formats.
ISBN 978-0-7787-4986-8 (hardcover).--
ISBN 978-0-7787-4999-8 (softcover).--ISBN 978-1-4271-2128-8 (HTML)

        1. Refugees--Guatemala--Juvenile literature. 2. Refugee children--
Guatemala--Juvenile literature. 3. Return migration--Guatemala--Juvenile
literature. 4. Repatriation--Guatemala--Juvenile literature. 5. Refugees--
Social conditions--Juvenile literature. 6. Refugees--Guatemala--Social
conditions--Juvenile literature. 7. Guatemala--Social conditions--
Juvenile literature. I. Title.

HV640.5.G9H833 2018   j305.9'06914097281   C2018-903021-6
                                                    C2018-903022-4

Library of Congress Cataloging-in-Publication Data

Crabtree Publishing Company
www.crabtreebooks.com   1-800-387-7650

Printed in the U.S.A./092018/CG20180719

Published in Canada
Crabtree Publishing
616 Welland Ave.
St. Catharines, Ontario
L2M 5V6

Published in the United States
Crabtree Publishing
PMB 59051
350 Fifth Avenue, 59th Floor
New York, New York 10118

Published in the United Kingdom
Crabtree Publishing
Maritime House
Basin Road North, Hove
BN41 1WR

Published in Australia
Crabtree Publishing
3 Charles Street
Coburg North
VIC, 3058

What Is in This Book?

Martinez's Story: From Mexico to Guatemala 4

My Homeland, Guatemala 6

Martinez's Story: Leaving My Homeland 8

A New Life 10

Martinez's Story: Coming Back Home 12

A New Home 14

Martinez's Story: My New Home................................. 16

A New School 18

Martinez's Story: A New Way of Learning.................... 20

Everything Changes 22

Martinez's Story: My New Way of Life 24

Martinez's Story: Looking to the Future...................... 26

Do Not Forget Our Stories! 28

Glossary 30

Learning More... 31

Index and About the Author 32

Martinez's Story: From Mexico to Guatemala

Hello! My name is Martinez. I am 11 years old. I came to Mexico as a **refugee** from Guatemala. Guatemala was not safe anymore. **Gangs** were becoming more powerful and were threatening violence. We were very afraid.

Mexico's flag

Guatemala's flag

There was a **civil war** in Guatemala from 1960 until 1996. After the war, many people lived in poverty.

One day, my brother Carlos and his friend Luis were shot at by some gang members. The gang wanted my brother to join, but he did not want to. Mamá said it was now too dangerous to stay in Guatemala.

A child's family has the **responsibility** to help ensure their **rights** are protected and to help them learn to exercise their rights. Think about these rights as you read this book.

I was born in Quetzaltenango. It is the second-largest city in Guatemala. There is a park in the center of the city and many museums, shops, and offices. The city is surrounded by beautiful mountains. One time, Mamá and I climbed to the top of Santa María Volcano. We could see all the way to Lake Atitlán. I loved living there. I was so upset when we had to leave. But it was the right thing to keep us safe.

Mexico

Belize

Guatemala

Honduras

El Salvador

Nicaragua

Guatemala, Honduras, and El Salvador together form an area called the **Northern Triangle.**

5

My Homeland, Guatemala

Guatemala has beautiful scenery and a rich **culture**. Many Guatemalans are mestizo. This means their **ancestors** are both Spanish and Mayan. Their clothing, food, customs, and buildings show signs of both cultures.

But there are a lot of problems in Guatemala. After the civil war ended, gangs began to form. Today, these powerful gangs control much of the country. Violence is a big problem. More than 4,500 people were killed by violent acts in 2017.

There is no strong police force to combat the gangs' activities. Most crimes are not even investigated. This private police officer was hired to protect a drinking water supply in Guatemala City.

Natural disasters have added to the difficulties. Between 2014 and 2016, there was not enough rain for crops to grow well. In 2017, strong winds, heavy rain, floods, and landslides damaged crops further. Now, millions of Guatemalans do not have enough food. These events and the violence have caused a **humanitarian crisis**.

Story in Numbers

In Guatemala,

2.1 million

people live in places where gangs have control. There are

14,000

gang members in Guatemala.

Many people leave Guatemala to seek **asylum** in safer places to live. Others choose to stay in the country. They hope their lives will one day get better. Some people do not have enough money to leave. Others do not want to leave friends and family behind. Many people are scared about what will happen after they leave. Life as a refugee is not easy.

People in poor areas of Guatemala often live in poverty. More than 60,000 people live in this cramped 1-mile-long (1.6 km) area in Guatemala City.

Martinez's Story: Leaving My Homeland

My family left Guatemala three years ago. We sold all our belongings to raise money to go to Mexico. My abuela (grandmother) made scarves to sell in a market to raise money. My two older brothers, Carlos and Maynor, helped a farmer with his crops before school and on weekends to earn more money.

Story in Numbers

14,596

people applied for asylum in Mexico in 2017. This is a 66 percent increase from 2016.

About 50 percent of Guatemalans work in agriculture.

Three months later, we still did not have enough money. But Mamá did not want to wait any longer. Carlos was threatened again by a gang. She borrowed money so that she could pay a **coyote** $35,000 to get us to Mexico.

We took a bus to a town where many coyotes live. Mamá found a coyote right away. She made a deal with him. For $5,000 for each person, he would help us get out of Guatemala.

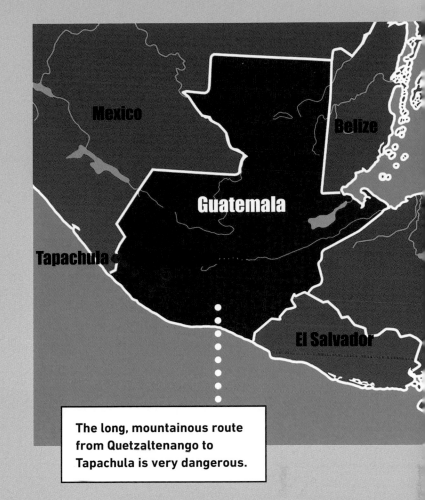

The long, mountainous route from Quetzaltenango to Tapachula is very dangerous.

It was a long, hard journey. We first traveled by bus, then crossed a river by boat. We walked the last part. But, finally, we made it to Tapachula, Mexico. We stayed there for 45 days. Then we heard we had been given asylum in Mexico! We moved to Mexico City.

These refugees are crossing the river from Guatemala to Mexico. Refugees can only travel safely to Mexico with the help of a coyote. Coyotes pay money to gangs and government officials to be allowed to travel on their lands.

A New Life

Building a new life in Mexico is not easy for most refugees. The Mexican Commission for Refugee Assistance (COMAR) deals with the refugees. But the COMAR officers are often poorly trained. There are huge numbers of refugees, so the officers talk many into not applying for asylum. Some wait in **detention centers**. These are a little like jails. Some refugees must stay there while their applications are processed. Others are not told about their right to apply for asylum. Instead, they are deported, or forced to leave the country.

Refugees who are granted asylum can look for jobs in Mexico. They have access to health care and can go to school. Most Guatemalan refugees feel safer in Mexico. They do not fear gang violence.

These Guatemalan refugees live in a shelter for migrant children in Mexico, near the border with Guatemala. There, they wait to find out if they will be given asylum in Mexico.

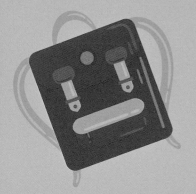

Mexico's International Organization for Migration (IOM) works to keep refugee children in school. It makes sure that they have access to school programs.

Some organizations help refugees build new lives in Mexico. Asylum Access Mexico (AAMX) offers free legal services near the Mexican border with Guatemala. It helps ensure refugees are safe and have the right to find work, get an education, and move around freely.

But it is still often hard for refugees to get jobs and find places to live. If they find work, the pay is usually very low. Some people **discriminate** against refugees. They refuse to help them or give them jobs.

Martinez's Story: Coming Back Home

We have spent nearly a year in Mexico. Life in Mexico is hard. Mamá has lost her job. She cannot find more work. We had a nice house in Guatemala. Now, we are living in a shack. We sleep on the ground. I hate to see how my abuela's back aches every morning. We are all miserable.

Guatemalan refugees seek safety in Mexico. But Mexico has its own problems. More than 34 million Mexicans live in poverty. People live in tiny apartments made from cardboard and reeds.

Last week, Mamá got a call from our Uncle Andres in Guatemala. Her sister, Aunt Sofia, is very sick. Uncle Andres is worried she might die. He cannot work and care for their three young children by himself. At first, Andres wanted to send the children to live with us in Mexico. But we cannot even feed ourselves properly. We could not feed three more people. Also, it is not safe for my cousins to travel alone to Mexico. They could be kidnapped or worse.

Around half of all Mexican children live in poverty. And each year, thousands more children flee to Mexico from the Northern Triangle, many without their parents.

Mamá did not know what to do. She and abuela talked for many days in hushed voices. Finally, she told us that we had to return to Guatemala. We needed to help our family. And life in Mexico was not improving.

Dear Juan,

I will miss you very much when we go back to Guatemala. Thank you for helping me learn to speak Spanish. I am scared to leave here. The trip home will be hard. Who knows what will happen when we arrive? All I can think about are the gangs and the trouble they caused for my family. I hope they do not find us. I wonder if I will ever feel safe again.

Your friend, Martinez

A New Home

Some refugees are sent back home before they reach Mexico. Others are deported, even when they have lived in Mexico for years. Some choose to return home. All of these **returnees** need help to rebuild their lives in Guatemala.

Many returnees do not have a place to live or any money. Some have been away for many years. They may have developed new skills in their **host country**. They may want to use those skills to find a job in Guatemala.

These Guatemalans are returnee families from Mexico. Here, they are walking away from church after a service. Being back in Guatemala can mean reconnecting with their culture.

UN Rights of the Child

You have the right to be protected from being hurt and mistreated, in body or mind.

These returnee children are enjoying player soccer, the top sport in Guatemala.

There is not much help available to returnees in Guatemala. A few organizations meet refugees at the airport or bus stations. They provide food and emergency shelter. They help refugees find family members. But most programs do not provide long-term help. They do not have enough money to do so.

Some organizations provide additional food and health care. World Vision offers arts and education programs to young people. Glasswing International provides education and medical care.

The Guatemalan government works with the Instituto Técnico de Capacitación y Productividad (INTECAP). This is a Guatemalan university. It offers job-training programs, such as cooking and tourism, to some refugees who return home. The training helps the returnees find jobs that pay better.

Martinez's Story: My New Home

We left Mexico about a year after we got the call from Uncle Andres. We took a bus to the Mexican border. It took us about five hours to get there. At the border, we showed our papers. People were waiting to enter or exit Guatemala. Vans and buses were honking their horns. It was very busy.

Finally, we made it across. We boarded another bus. It was crammed full of people. Some riders even rode on top in their closed vehicles. For most of the way to my uncle's village, farmland surrounded us. It was a small community. There are about 300 people living there.

Colorful buses like this in Guatemala are called chicken buses.

Dear Juan,
Inside this envelope, you will find a picture from my journey back home to Guatemala. I found an old camera in a shop before we left. Carlos and Maynor bought it for me. We spent most of the journey on buses. Even my abuela is ok. She was tired and sore after the long journey. But she stayed positive. I will send you some more pictures so you can see the farm where I live now. My cousins and I have a lot of fun feeding the chickens! I miss you.
Martinez

I am sad we cannot go back to our old house in Quetzaltenango. I want to see my old friends so badly. But I know it is for the best. The gang would come after us if we went back there. No one wants that to happen.

This small farm is in the north of Guatemala. Bananas, coffee, palm oil, and sugar are some of Guatemala's main crops.

UN Rights of the Child

You have the right to practice your own language, culture, and religion, and to choose your own friends.

A New School

The government puts a lot of money into Guatemala's schools. There are primary schools, secondary schools, and universities. By law, children must go to primary school for at least six years from the age of 7 to 14.

Public primary schools are free to attend. The government pays for teachers' wages, textbooks, and meals at primary schools. Still, many poor families cannot afford to send their children to school because they cannot pay for school supplies. Many schools also ask parents for extra money to pay for wage increases, school repairs, and drinking water.

Only about 75 percent of students complete their primary education in Guatemala.

At some schools in Guatemala, children help clean and take care of the building.

Many Guatemalan schools require students to wear a uniform. If parents cannot afford a uniform, it can prevent children from attending school.

Children do not have to go to school after the sixth grade. Many do not attend secondary school at all. This is because most secondary schools are in bigger cities. It is hard for **rural** students to get to them. Many need to stay home to help on the farm.

There is one public university in Guatemala. It is free to attend, but students must pay their own living expenses. Many cannot afford to do so. It is very hard to get in. Students must have good grades, pass a special test, and speak Spanish.

UN Rights of the Child

You have the right to a good quality education. You should be encouraged to go to school to the highest level you can.

Martinez's Story: A New Way of Learning

I could not go to school for the first few weeks we were back in Guatemala. There was too much farm work for Uncle Andres to do by himself. I stayed home from school to help. Now, I go to school most days. Uncle Andres still needs me to help sometimes. Many of the boys my age have dropped out to help at home. I think about dropping out, too. Then I could get a job and help pay the bills. Mamá wants me to stay in school. She has big dreams for me.

In Guatemala, 90 percent of schools do not have books.

Most families in my new community have a lot of kids. Many can only afford to send one child to school. My little sister Emely goes to school only a few days each month. She helps Mamá and my abuela around the house. Maynor and Carlos got jobs building a road in town. The money they make helps put food on our table.

On average, Guatemalan children attend school for only 3.5 years.

My school is small. There are not enough books to go around. It is hard to get good teachers in some places. My teacher only speaks Spanish. Many of the kids in my class only speak the local language, like I used to. I help them whenever I can. I learned Spanish in Mexico.

Dear Juan,

Can you believe I am the best Spanish speaker in my class? I was not good compared to the other kids in Mexico. But I have you to thank for helping me learn the language. I sure miss our classes together. We were so lucky to have computers and books to use. My classroom has way too many kids. It is very cramped. I sit at a pile of bricks instead of at a desk. And we have no computers.

Write soon,

Martinez

Everything Changes

Refugees often return to the same or worse conditions than when they left Guatemala. The government remains dishonest. The police cannot be trusted. Violent crime takes place often.

Returning home causes complicated feelings for refugees. They may feel badly, as though they failed to build a new life. They may experience anger and fear. Some have nightmares about their experiences. Some Guatemalans believe that returning refugees were deported because they did something wrong. They may treat deported returnees with discrimination.

These Guatemalans are trying to find anything of value in the garbage. Around 40 percent of Guatemalans live on less than $1.50 a day.

Returnee Guatemalans must try to find work wherever they can, but this can be very difficult. Even if they do find work, pay is often low. Guatemalan farmers, for example, earn $3 to $4 a day.

The government has a responsibility to make sure your rights are protected. They must help your family to protect your rights, and create an environment where you can grow and reach your potential.

There is still a lot of violence against children in Guatemala. Charities such as **UNICEF** work hard to protect children's rights there.

Returning to Guatemala is a big change—even if it is the homeland of a refugee. They often had different ways of living in their host country. Children and adults may need **counseling**. This helps them cope with their new lives in their homeland. Without assistance to such as counseling, returnees are more likely to feel alone and struggle to make a new life. This sometimes makes them **vulnerable** to gangs, who look for new members.

Martinez's Story: My New Way of Life

Many years ago, my Uncle Andres worked in the United States. He was deported after three years. But he did make some money while he was there. He bought a small piece of land on the side of a mountain. It has good soil. It is perfect for growing beans, corn, and vegetables.

We have had bad weather recently. It has made it harder to grow crops. So to make more money, we sell the eggs that our chickens lay.

Poor families need children to work in the fields for money. Some charities, such as Cooperative for Education, help children stay in school and gain their high school diploma.

Volcan de Fuego is a very active volcano. Although it is very dangerous, the volcano has made the soil around it good for growing crops.

Pedro, mi amigo (my friend)!

Juan sent me a letter a few weeks ago. He told me your family had tried to move to the United States. He said you were separated from your parents at the border. Is it true you were sent to a care center on the other side of the country? You must have been so scared! Juan said it was a long time before your parents were able to call you. I'm so glad you were finally brought back together. But I was sad to hear you were all sent back to Mexico. I know you were hoping to move in with your aunt in California. I hope you make it there someday. I know what it feels like to try to move to a new place. I hope you are well.

Your friend,

Martinez

Story in Numbers

In Guatemala,

50 percent

of children under the age of five do not have enough food to grow big and strong.

*Our house has two floors. It is about one hour's walk away from Uncle Andres' farm. Some days, when I am not at school, I carry heavy jugs of **fertilizer** and water to the farm. It is hard work, but it has to be done. Uncle Andres says if we have a good crop this year, we can buy a small truck for the farm. That will be a big help! At least we have a bicycle that we all share for trips into town. I sometimes ride it to my friend Pablo's house. We play* cincos *(marbles) or* chamuscas *(street soccer).*

Martinez's Story: Looking to the Future

When we first got to San Jose Calderas, I worried all the time. I was scared that the gang that was after my brother would find us. But now I feel safer. Our neighbors are all very friendly. Everyone looks out for one another. I even like helping my uncle on the farm.

Guatemalan women are known for their traditional weaving skills. They make colorful items such as shawls, tablecloths, and towels.

More than 50 percent of the population in Guatemala is under the age of 19.

UN Rights of the Child

You have the right to play and rest.

My aunt gets stronger every day. Mamá has started a tour guide training program. When she is done, she will take people on hikes up Acatenango Volcano. Guides earn four times as much money as farmers! She will be able to pay for both me and Emely to go to school all the time.

I dream of one day going to university. I want to be a doctor and help people, like my aunt, when they are sick. My abuela is saving money to help pay for my secondary school. I still worry about our future, though. If the gangs come here, we might have to leave. But where would we go then?

Juan, Pedro, Francisco, and Jorge, I found a shop in town that has a pretty good Internet connection. At last! It is so hard to get online in Guatemala. Mamá is starting work for a local tour company in a few months. Maybe you can take one of her tours one day. The hike takes you all the way to the top of Acatenango Volcano, where you can watch the sunrise. It is so beautiful. I hope we get to stay here. How is everything in Mexico?
Martinez

Think you can make it to the top?

Do Not Forget Our Stories!

Refugees flee their countries out of fear and in search of safety. They may be forced to leave. They hope to build a new, better life in another country.

Sometimes, refugees return to their homeland. Refugees who return home often face difficult conditions. They may not have a place to live. Many have lived through very upsetting experiences. Sometimes, the community does not accept them. Still, refugees are strong. They work hard to rebuild their lives and are important parts of their communities. They bring special skills and add to their local cultures by sharing such things as their food, traditions, art, and music. Most adult refugees in new countries have jobs and support their new country by paying **taxes**. They often help support other newcomers in their communities, too.

With the help of the **United Nations High Commissioner for Refugees (UNHCR)**, many Guatemalans are opening their homes to people on the move. These shelters offer food, a safe place to stay, and information about refugee rights.

UN Rights of the Child

You have the right to choose your own friends and join or set up groups, as long as it is not harmful to others.

Refugee stories are not always in the news. It is important to remember that there are hundreds of thousands of refugees in all parts of the world. You can help by keeping their stories alive.

Guatemalans hope for a peaceful country in which they can safely raise their families.

Discussion Prompts

1. Why do some refugees return to their homeland?
2. What are some of the challenges Guatemalan refugees face when they arrive back in their homeland?
3. What types of support are available for refugees returning to Guatemala?

Glossary

ancestors People in your family from long ago

asylum Protection given to refugees by a country

civil war A war between groups of people in the same country

counseling Giving advice about personal problems

coyote A person who illegally moves Latin Americans across borders for a high fee

culture The shared beliefs, values, traditions, arts, and ways of life of a group of people

detention centers Places where people are kept until the government decides where they should go

discriminate Treat unfairly or differently based on someone's gender, race, religion, or other identifiers

fertilizer Chemicals used to help plants grow

gangs Organized groups of criminals

host country A country that offers to give refugees a home

humanitarian crisis An event that brings harm to the health, safety, and well-being of a large group of people

justice system The system that decides whether someone has broken the law

refugee A person who flees from his or her own country to another due to unsafe conditions

responsibility The duty to deal with something

returnees People who have returned to a place they had left

rights Privileges and freedoms protected by law

rural Of or from the countryside

taxes An amount of money paid to a government for services, such as education

UNICEF United Nations Children's Fund; a global organization that defends and protects the rights of children

United Nations High Commissioner for Refugees (UNHCR) A program that protects and supports refugees everywhere

vulnerable At risk of harm

Learning More

Books

Diaz, Alexandra. *The Only Road.* Simon & Schuster, 2017.

O'Brien, Anne Sibley. *I'm New Here.* Charlesbridge Publishing, 2015.

Sheehan, Sean, and Magdalene Koh. *Guatemala* (Cultures of the World). Cavendish Square, 2018.

Websites

https://kids.nationalgeographic.com/explore/countries/guatemala
Visit this website for facts and pictures about Guatemala.

www.unicef.org/rightsite/files/uncrcchilldfriendlylanguage.pdf
Explore the United Nations Convention on the Rights of the Child.

www.unrefugees.org/news/central-america-s-children-on-the-run
Find out how children are affected by gang violence in the Northern Triangle.

Index

asylum seekers 7, 8, 9, 10, 11

children 10, 11, 13, 14, 18–19, 20–21, 23, 24, 25, 26
civil war 4, 6
coyotes 9

deportation 10, 13, 14, 22, 24

farm work 8, 17, 19, 20, 22, 24, 25, 26, 27

gangs 4, 6, 7, 9, 10, 13, 17, 23, 26, 27
going to Mexico 9, 10–11, 12–13

helping refugees 10, 11, 15, 23, 28, 29

jobs 8, 10, 11, 12, 14, 15, 20, 22, 27

leaving Guatemala 4, 5, 6–7, 8–9

map 5
Martinez's story 4–5, 8–9, 12–13, 16–17, 20–21, 24–25, 26–27

Northern Triangle 5, 13

poverty 4, 7, 12, 13, 20, 21, 22

returnees 14–15, 16–17, 22–23

schools 11, 18–19, 20–21, 24, 27
sharing stories 28–29
shelters 10, 15, 28

UN Rights of the Child 5, 11, 14, 17, 19, 23, 26, 29

volcanoes 5, 24, 27

About the Author

Heather C. Hudak travels all over the world and loves to learn about different cultures. She has been to more than 50 countries, from Brazil to Indonesia and many others in between. When she is not on the road, she enjoys spending time with her dog named Mouse and cat named Turtle.